Knights & Castles

Jane Walker
Consultant: Richard Tames

Miles
Kelly
PUBLISHING

First published in 2002 by
Miles Kelly Publishing Ltd
Bardfield Centre, Great Bardfield, Essex, CM7 4SL

Some material in this book can also be found in *100 Things You Should Know About Knights and Castles.*

Editor: Amanda Learmonth

Design: Debbie Meekcoms

Index: Lynn Bresler

Art Director: Clare Sleven

Editorial Director: Paula Borton

British Library Cataloguing-in-Publication Data
A catalogue record for this book is available from the British Library

ISBN 1-84236-106-6

Printed in Hong Kong

www.mileskelly.net
info@mileskelly.net

ACKNOWLEDGEMENTS

The Publishers would like to thank the following artists who have contributed to this book:

Richard Berridge (Specs Art), Vanessa Card, Nicholas Forder, Mike Foster (Maltings Partnership), Terry Gabbey (AFA), Luigi Galante (Studio Galante), Sally Holmes, Richard Hook (Linden Artists), John James (Temple Rogers), Andy Lloyds Jones, Janos Marffy, Angus McBride, Terry Riley, Nik Spender (Advocate), Roger Stewart, Rudi Vizi, Mike White (Temple Rogers)

Computer-generated cartoons by James Evans

Contents

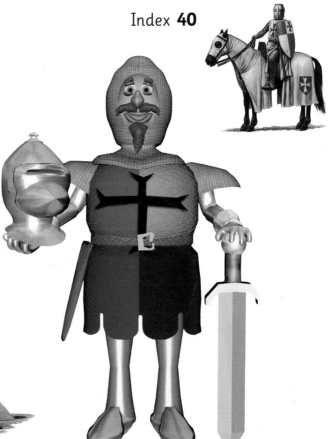

Life in the Middle Ages

In the Middle Ages, between the years 470 and 1450, many castles and forts were built. A castle provided shelter for a king or a lord and his family, and helped him to defend his lands.

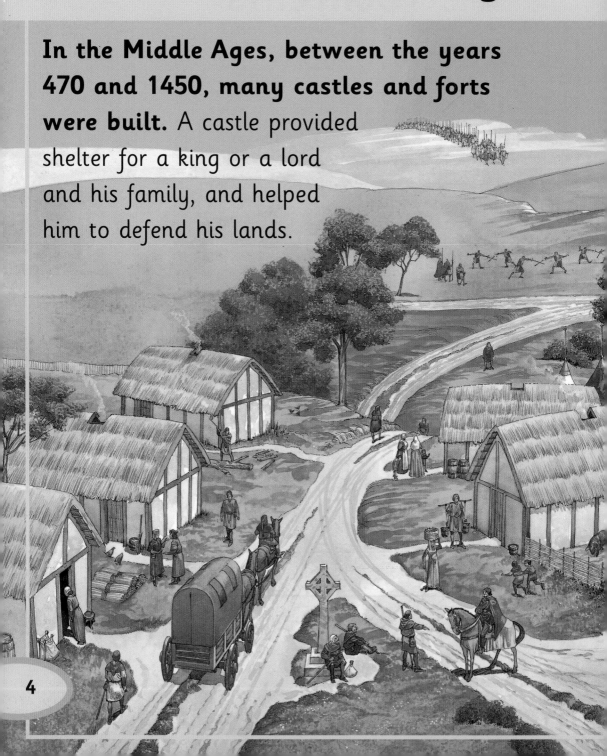

Soldiers practised their fighting skills in the castle grounds.

Knights were soldiers who fought on horseback.

Peasants farmed the land around the castle.

5

The first castles

The first castles were mostly built from wood. But they were not very strong and caught fire easily, so from around 1100 onwards, people began to build castles in stone. A stone castle gave better protection against attack, fire, cold and rainy weather.

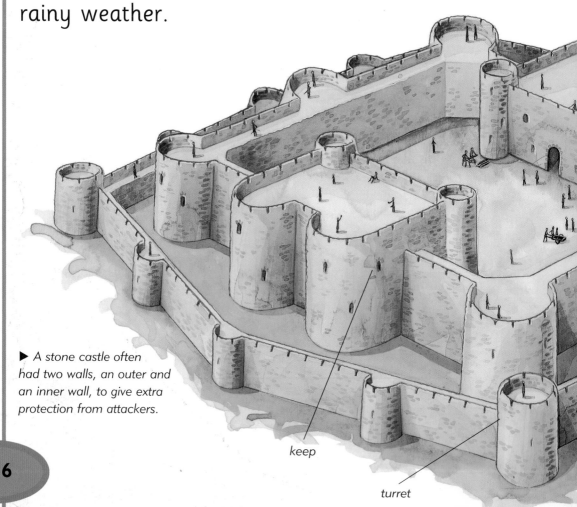

▶ A stone castle often had two walls, an outer and an inner wall, to give extra protection from attackers.

keep

turret

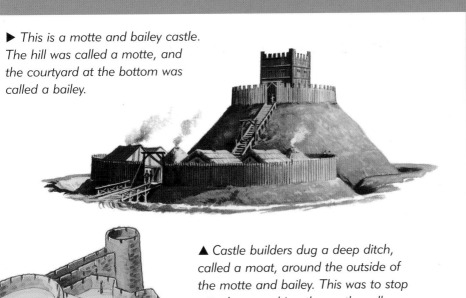

▶ This is a motte and bailey castle. The hill was called a motte, and the courtyard at the bottom was called a bailey.

▲ Castle builders dug a deep ditch, called a moat, around the outside of the motte and bailey. This was to stop attackers reaching the castle walls.

gatehouse

inner defensive wall

outer defensive wall

Archers stood on the castle walls and fired down at enemies.

Japanese castles were built with different layers.

Lancelot's fun facts!

The builders of the early wooden castles covered the walls with wet leather – to stop them from burning down.

Building castles

The best place to build a castle was on top of a hill. A hilltop position gave good views over the surrounding countryside and so made it harder for an enemy to launch a surprise attack.

Workers who built the walls were called roughmasons

A giant wheel was used to lift heavy stones

Castle walls *had to be thick and strong.*

The keep *was the safest part of the castle, where the lord lived.*

A master mason *controlled the building of the castle.*

9

Inside the castle

Stone castles were cold, damp places. Cold winds blew through the windows, which had no glass. There was no heating or running water.

Castle quiz

1. When were the Middle Ages?

2. What was the courtyard at the bottom of a castle called?

3. What were the first castles made of?

4. What is the name of the ditch that surrounds a castle?

1. between 470 and 1450 2. the bailey 3. wood 4. a moat

▼ *Castles were kept warm by fires burning in huge fireplaces.*

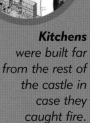

Kitchens *were built far from the rest of the castle in case they caught fire.*

Dungeons *were dark, slimy prisons.*

Tapestries *on the walls helped to warm the rooms.*

Castle life

A castle was the home of an important and powerful person, such as a king, a lord or a knight. The lord controlled the castle itself, as well as the lands and people around it. The lady of the castle was in charge of the day-to-day running.

▼ Local villagers were allowed to shelter inside the castle walls when their lands were under attack.

▶ The lord and lady gave orders to the knights, servants and peasants.

The steward was in charge of all the servants.

◀ The master of the horse had to look after the lord's horses.

Servants cooked, cleaned and and ran errands.

Lancelot's fun facts!

There was no bathroom for the castle's servants. They had to take a dip in the local river to wash – and to get rid of any fleas and lice!

People and power

In the Middle Ages, the king or queen was the most important person in the country. The king gave land to his barons and other noblemen. In return, they supplied the king with soldiers and weapons to fight wars. This system of giving away land in return for services was known as feudalism.

Castle quiz

1. Who was in charge of the castle?
2. Who was in charge of the servants?
3. Why were there tapestries on the castle walls?
4. Which room was built far away from the other rooms in case it caught fire?

1. the lord and lady 2. the steward 3. to keep the rooms warm 4. the kitchen

▲ In the Middle Ages, the Church and the ruler of the country were both very powerful, so they had to try to work together.

Barons *were the most powerful of all noblemen.*

Knights *defended the king and lords from their enemies.*

Peasants *were the very poorest people.*

15

Knight school

It took about 14 years of training to become a knight. A boy started to learn to be a knight at around the age of seven. He was taught how to ride and shoot a bow and arrow. He then became a squire, or assistant, where he learned how to fight with a sword. If he was good enough, he became a knight at 21.

◀ The ceremony of making a new knight was known as dubbing. A knight had to pray all night in church before his dubbing ceremony took place.

A sword with two sharp edges like this was used by knights in the Middle Ages.

◀ During the dubbing ceremony, a knight was tapped on the shoulder with a sword.

A mace was a metal club with deadly spikes.

Lancelot's fun facts!

Shoes with pointed toes were popular with French knights. But when they needed to make a quick escape in battle, they had to cut the points off to run away!

War games

Knights often took part in mock battles called tournaments. Tournaments were good practice for the real thing – war. Knights divided into two sides and fought each other as if in a proper battle.

▶ Jousts were watched by ladies of the court as well as ordinary people. Knights could show off their skills and bravery to impress them.

Coats of arms were badges worn by knights so others could recognise them in battle.

◀ Jousting was a fight between two knights on horseback. Each knight tried to win by knocking the other off his horse.

Banners displayed a knight's own personal design.

Lancelot's fun facts!

Some knights cheated in jousts by wearing special armour that was fixed on to the horse's saddle!

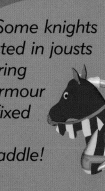

Dress for battle

Early knights wore a type of armour called chainmail. It was made of thousands of tiny iron rings joined on to each other. Gradually, knights began to wear more and more armour, until by the 1400s, they were wearing full suits of steel armour.

▼ Knights had two main weapons: the sword and the shield. But they also fought with lances (long wooden spears), daggers and axes.

A wool tunic was worn over the top of a knight's armour.

Chainmail was a kind of 'knitted' metal armour.

Lancelot's fun facts!

Soldiers called 'retrievers' used to have to run into the middle of the battle and collect up all the spare arrows!

Famous battles

On and off between 1337 and 1453, England and France were at war. This was called the Hundred Years' War. The two countries fought each other to decide who should control France. In the end the French won, and England lost all of her lands in France except for the port of Calais.

▼ *In 1429, a young French girl called Joan of Arc led the French army to victory against the English.*

▲ *The Bayeux tapestry tells the story of the Norman invasion of England in 1066. William of Normandy, known as William the Conqueror, invaded England and defeated Harold, the English king, at the Battle of Hastings.*

William the Conqueror *claimed that he was promised the throne of England.*

Knights *fought many bloody battles in the Hundred Years' War.*

Lancelot's fun facts!

If you captured a knight alive during battle, you could offer him back to his family in return for a generous amount of money!

Brave knights

Many famous stories, or legends, have been written about knights and their bravery.
The legend of St George tells how he killed a fierce dragon. King Arthur became king after pulling a magic sword, called Excalibur, out of a stone. Lancelot, Arthur's favourite knight, fell in love with Arthur's wife, Guinevere.

Knight quiz

1. What was the ceremony of making a new knight called?

2. Which two countries fought a war that lasted around 100 years?

3. What were a knight's two main weapons in battle?

4. Who did William the Conqueror defeat in the Battle of Hastings?

1. dubbing 2. France and England 3. sword and shield 4. King Harold

El Cid
was a Spanish
knight who
fought against
the Moors of
North Africa.

**The Black
Prince**
was a great
English warrior.

King Arthur
had followers
called the
Knights of the
Round Table.

▲ St George was
adopted as the patron saint
of England in the 1300s.

25

Love and poetry

Musicians of the Middle Ages, called minstrels, sang songs and recited poetry about love and bravery. These songs and poems showed knights as faithful and religious men who were prepared to die for their king or lord. In real life, knights did not always live up to this ideal picture.

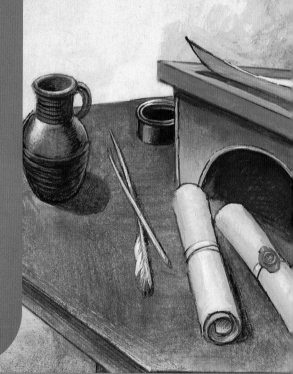

Illuminated letter

An illuminated letter is the first letter of a song or poem, decorated with pictures and patterns.

Create your own illuminated letter for the first letter of your name:

Draw the outline in fine black pen. Use pens or paints to decorate it.

▼ Troubadours were poet-musicians who composed songs about heroic knights and ideal love.

Minstrels sang songs while playing an instrument called a lute.

Secret letters were written by a knight to the woman he loved.

A wax seal was pressed on to the letter as the knight's own personal mark.

27

Great feasts

The great hall was the centre of castle life. The lord and his family ate their meals here and carried out their daily business. Huge feasts, called banquets, were also held here. Vast amounts of fancy food, such as stuffed swan and wild boar, were served.

Bake a 'tarte of apples'

You will need: a packet of shortcrust pastry, 8 eating apples, $1/2$ cup of brown sugar, $1/2$ teaspoon cinnamon, pinch of dried ginger, a little milk

- Ask an adult to help you. Line a pie dish with pastry and bake for 10 minutes in a medium-hot oven.
- Peel, core and slice the apples. Mix them with the sugar, cinnamon and ginger. Layer the apples in the dish.
- Place a pastry lid over the top and brush with a little milk. Make small slits in the lid. Bake in a medium-hot oven for about 45 minutes.

Wild boar's head was often served at banquets.

◄ Jesters, jugglers and acrobats entertained the diners at banquets.

Fine wine was drunk by important guests out of proper glasses.

Fruit and nuts were eaten for dessert, as well as fruit pies and jellies.

Fighting back

When the enemy was spotted approaching a castle, its defenders first pulled up the castle drawbridge. They also lowered an iron grate, called a portcullis, to form an extra barrier behind the drawbridge.

Castle quiz

1. What is the name of a musician from the Middle Ages?

2. Where in a castle were banquets held?

3. Which saint killed a fierce dragon in the famous legend?

4. What were King Arthur's followers called?

1. a minstrel
2. the Great Hall 3. St George
4. Knights of the Round Table

Boiling water was poured on to enemy heads.

A battering ram was a wooden hut which gave protection from enemy fire.

Heavy stones were thrown on to the enemy below.

The Crusades

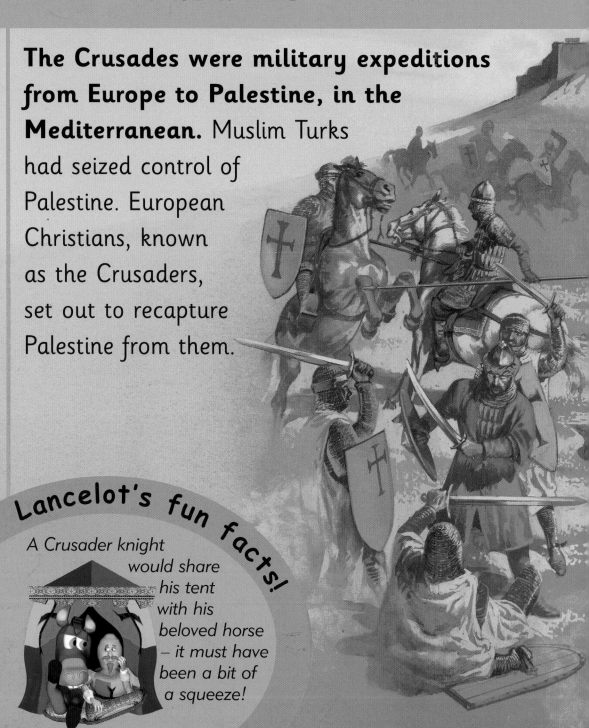

The Crusades were military expeditions from Europe to Palestine, in the Mediterranean. Muslim Turks had seized control of Palestine. European Christians, known as the Crusaders, set out to recapture Palestine from them.

Lancelot's fun facts!

A Crusader knight would share his tent with his beloved horse – it must have been a bit of a squeeze!

Knights and castles

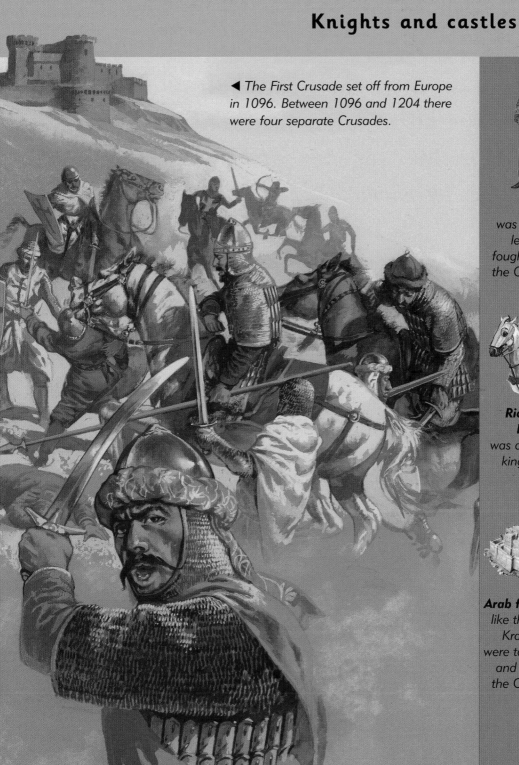

◄ The First Crusade set off from Europe in 1096. Between 1096 and 1204 there were four separate Crusades.

Saladin was a Muslim leader who fought against the Crusaders.

Richard the Lionheart was an English king who led the Third Crusade.

Arab fortresses like this one at Krak in Syria were taken over and rebuilt by the Crusaders.

Castle siege

A siege is when an enemy surrounds a castle and stops all supplies from reaching the people inside. The idea is to starve them until they surrender or die.

The belfry was used for firing directly at the battlements.

▶ This machine was called a trebuchet. It had a long wooden arm with a sling. A heavy stone was placed inside the sling which was thrown towards the castle walls.

A crossbow was a more accurate weapon than a bow and arrow.

◀ A risky way of trying to get inside a castle was to climb over the walls.

A longbow could fire from a long way away.

Wooden shields protected the archers from enemy fire

Lancelot's fun facts!

The ropes used to wind up trebuchet machines were made from plaits of human hair!

Eastern warriors

Warrior knights in Japan during the Middle Ages were known as samurai. The samurai, like European knights, usually fought on horseback but later on they began to fight more on foot. Other Eastern warriors included the fierce Mongols, and the Seljuk Turks who conquered many lands.

▼ Mongol warriors terrified the enemy in battle. They were skilled horsemen who controlled their horses with their feet while standing up in the stirrups.

Samurai warriors wore metal armour fixed to padded silk or leather.

A curved samurai sword was a samurai warrior's most important possession.

Lancelot's fun facts!

The Turks fought with gold pieces in their mouth – to stop the Crusader knights from stealing their gold!

Famous castles

Many castles are said to be haunted by the ghosts of people who died within their walls. Many of these ghosts are kings and queens who were killed by their sworn enemies. Edward II of England was murdered in his cell at Berkeley Castle in southwest England. Richard II died at Pontefract Castle in Yorkshire.

▶ *This fairy-tale castle of Neuschwanstein was the dream project of 'mad' King Ludwig of Bavaria. Work started on it in 1869.*

▼ Visitors to Berkeley Castle say they can hear the screams of the murdered Edward at night.

▼ The town of Carcassonne in southern France is like one huge castle. It is surrounded by high walls and towers that were built in the Middle Ages.

Windsor castle has been the home of English kings and queens for over 900 years.

Glamis castle in Scotland is the scene for the Shakespeare play, *Macbeth*.

Bodiam Castle in England was built in the 1300s to keep out French armies.

Index